For Your Inspiration… Modern Poems

"Do what you can, with what you have, where you are."

—Theodore Roosevelt

I was amazed to learn of Mīchol's passion for poetry so late in his life. You will be captivated by his clever, yet profound expressions of the happy and painful realities of our world, as I was. Well done, brother!

—Luddy Zampier

"It's never too late to be what you might've been."

—George Eliot, pen name (Mary Ann Evans)

Grandma Moses began her career in painting in her 70's. So too, Mīchol began his career in crafting poems in his 70's. His sheer talent, combined with honesty, simplicity, humor, and insight is a delight. A good read!

—Adelaide Waring

"You don't need to see the whole staircase, just take the first step."

—Martin Luther King, Jr.

Modern Poems

MĪCHOL

ISBN 979-8-88751-667-7 (paperback)
ISBN 979-8-88832-680-0 (hardcover)
ISBN 979-8-88751-668-4 (digital)

Christian Faith Publishing
832 Park Avenue
Meadville, PA 16335
www.christianfaithpublishing.com

Printed in the United States of America

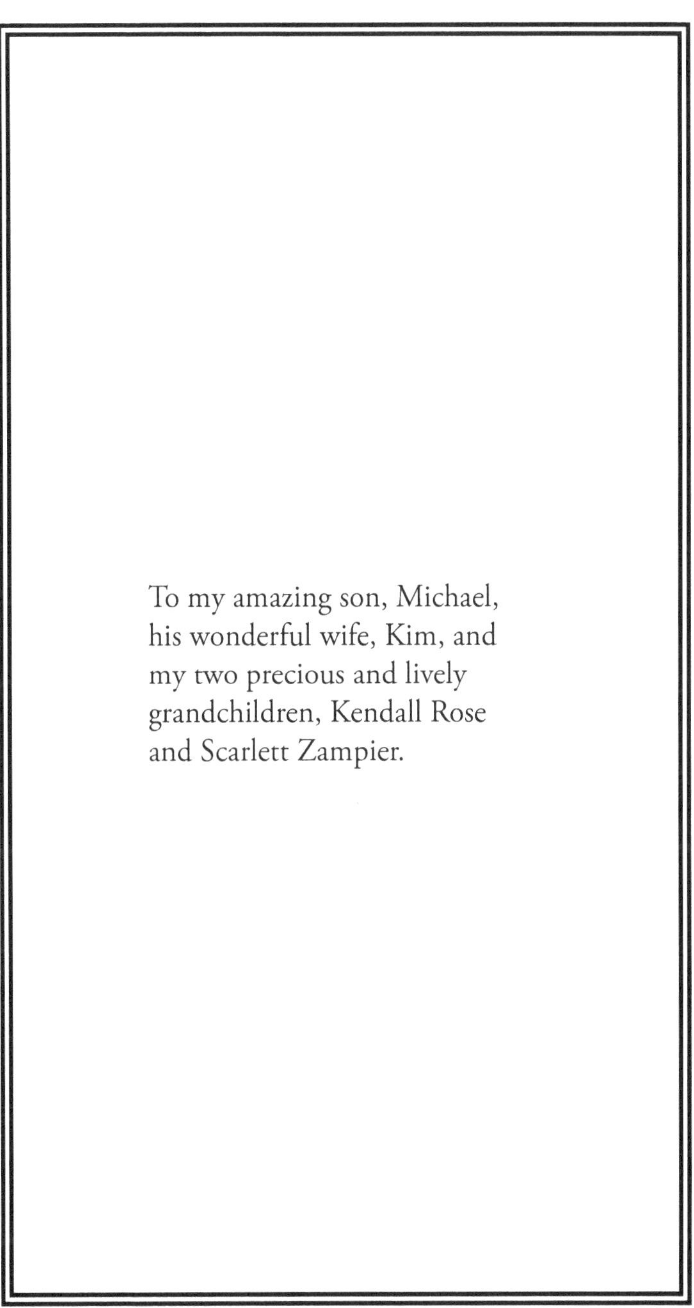

To my amazing son, Michael,
his wonderful wife, Kim, and
my two precious and lively
grandchildren, Kendall Rose
and Scarlett Zampier.

Contents

Christmas

Snowflakes fall on a chimney above.
Soft, cold, and sprinkled with love.

Family gathers round an evergreen tree.
How much their love so precious to me!

Turkey adorns the holiday table.
Men watch football on the cable.

Women tackle dinner dishes.
Children give thanks for Christmas wishes.

Everyone has their special reason.
All agree it's a wonderful season.

Let's all remember what this day is about.
Our Savior was born, there is no doubt.

New Year's Eve

Waiting all year for this exciting night.
Last year's dreams are out of sight.
Come what may for the New Year,
Hoping for good things feels just right.

Champagne bubbles make good cheer.
A sincere toast for those we hold dear.
Hugs and kisses feel so good.
With hopes and dreams, we have nothing to fear.

Fireworks explode in the winter sky,
Like a scene from the 4th of July.
Goosebumps abound on this festive night,
As we say "so long" to days gone by.

A chilly nip in the midnight air,
Shed a tear I just may dare.
Now's the time for the ball to drop
In old New York's Times Square.

Valentine's Day

Candy, flowers, a hug and a kiss,
Empty-handed I'd be remiss.

I'm so glad she is mine.
I only have one valentine.
She is very precious and sweet,
So, I walk the line and don't miss a beat.

On the town for dinner and a dance,
Adding gusto to our romance.

On this night the champagne is pink.
We lock our arms and take a drink.

I'll present her with a diamond ring.
She'll know it's not just a fling.

If she were to become my wife,
Surely we'd have a wonderful life.

St. Patrick's Day

In the month of March there's a holiday
We all enjoy… St. Patrick's Day.
Remember to wear something green.
We're all Irish, so let's make a scene.

There's a parade in every city.
To miss out would be a pity.

Love to visit the Emerald Isle.
Maybe stay for a while.

Wee leprechauns running wild;
Nothing to fear, they're quite mild.

Rolling hills of brilliant green,
Prettiest vista you've ever seen.

Patrick is their patron saint.
Portraits done in oil paint.

When I kiss the Blarney Stone,
Remembering not to be alone.

An Irish jig is always fun.
Celtics tout it's the only one.

After getting out of my tub,
Going to grace an Irish pub.

When I arrive there's no doubt,
Sure to order a Guinness stout.

Spring

Gradual melting of February's ice,
Warmer weather feels so nice.

Colorful tulips, the first to arrive;
Makes a body feel alive.

See the daisies and the daffodils.
A burst of color paves the hills.

A babbling brook, a country stream,
A gentle rain begins to teem.

Morning sky glows with red.
Pretty good reason to get outta bed.

Robins and sparrows perform their song.
Makes us want to sing along.

Spring has arrived we can assume,
As we say so long to winter's gloom.

Cherry Blossom Time

In the spring once a year,
Washingtonians have something to cheer.
A city-wide festival;
Music and laughter is all you'll hear.

Colorful blossoms of the cherry tree;
Everywhere you look it's all you see.
Concerts and parades in the street;
Exactly where I want to be.

Our former enemy wanted to appease.
The trees were a gift from the Japanese.
We now consider Japan a friend.
D.C. sites are around every bend.

Wanderlust

Wanderlust is a fun pastime.
All day long doesn't cost a dime.
When I reach that distant place,
City bells are sure to chime.

I love my family and my home.
I've always had a yearn to roam;
Crossing the prairies and the mountains
Just to see the Pacific foam.

Nowadays you can travel to space;
A tribute to the human race.
It may be a dangerous trip.
I'll ask my Lord for His saving grace.

Now you know what makes me tick;
Another hobby I could pick.
Just one polite request…
Please don't ever call me Mick.

Easter

Holy, Holy, Glory, Glory!
It's the world's greatest story.

Last week He walked on palms.
Of eminent danger, He had no qualms.

A crown of thorns, a cross to bear;
To lend a hand, no one would dare.

A nail in His foot, a nail in His hand;
A trickle of blood reached the sand.

A giant stone guards a cave.
It's our Lord's temporary grave.
In the morning, the room was empty.
Just the way it was meant to be.

Jesus accomplished His holy mission.
All His plans came to fruition.

Everyone's heart had reached its pinnacle.
Our Savior has performed His greatest miracle.

Easter for Kids

Once a year on an April Sunday,
All Christians take time to pray.

Where oh where can those eggs be?
I've looked everywhere I can see.
Before I cried, Mommy helped out.
And now I'm as happy as I can be.

Shortly after the egg contest,
Mommy asked me to wear my Sunday best.
Every Sunday we go to church.
Later on, there's a yummy feast.

A girl wore an Easter bonnet,
With pretty ribbons sewn upon it.

We kids know it's no ordinary Sunday.
We join the adults to kneel and pray.

Mother's Day

Our celebration will be positively gay,
Smack-dab in the middle of May.
To say it's special is an understatement.
Of course, we know it's Mother's Day.

She thanked us for the flowers and confection.
Mom especially enjoyed our love and affection.

An outdoor cafe sounds just right.
Mom was asked to bring her appetite.
So great to have family and friends.
She was satisfied from the very first bite.

Memorial Day

It comes every year in the last week of May.
More exact, it's always on Monday.
The unofficial first day of summer;
Who would think that's a bummer?

Thousands of mothers are still bawlin'
For their brave sons who have fallen.

Losing one war made us sad,
But nine out of ten isn't bad.

Noble soldiers gave the ultimate sacrifice,
Defending our country at any price.

How about a visit to Arlington?
…the largest cemetery in the nation.

One of the places we feel our grief.
Honoring those who passed is our belief.

We all owe a debt of gratitude.
Reverently remembering beckons a blessed mood.

Coffins cloaked with American flags,
Presenting loved ones with precious dog tags.

Military

There's the Army, Navy, and Marines.
You'll be accepted when you reach your late teens.

We also have the Coast Guard and Air Force.
Ask me if they're important; I'd say, of course.

The first stop is boot camp,
Easily found off the correct ramp.

Bivouac is an important part of training;
Going on maneuvers even if it's raining.

We shouldn't ignore their bravery
For defending our great country.

They are proud for choosing this.
Their former life they don't miss.

These brave men don't need to be smart,
As long as they have a sense of duty in their heart.

The meals they're served may be nutritious.
They don't reach the level of delicious.

Let's not forget the dutiful women.
They're as important; that's a given.

Some long for military action.
It's probably a small fraction.

If they're faced with a hostile act,
They're highly trained to react.

We celebrate these courageous soldiers on
        Veterans Day.
For those who gave the ultimate sacrifice,
We reverently observe Memorial Day.

Father's Day

You're really not going to give him a tie.
Suppose you could bake an apple pie.
We're talking about the man who raised you.
He's got to be your favorite guy.

This is the day to show affection.
Don't hand him a box of confection.
He's never not looked out for you;
Always shown you the right direction.

Cook him one of his favorite meals.
Buy him a new set of wheels.
We all say Happy Father's Day!
So why not seal the deal?

He loves his entire brood.
You gotta say he's a pretty cool dude.
Do some very nice things,
And put him in a great mood.

Newlyweds

It was love at first sight.
They decided to do what felt right.
After a happy and fun-filled courtship,
Things moved along at quite a fast clip.

Once up on the altar,
Quite confident neither would falter.

The priest was very courteous.
Both felt this ceremony was fabulous.

Recited their vows with sincerity.
Suiting their guests to a T.

The bride wore a magnificent gown.
Surely, the loveliest woman in town.

They married in the month of June.
It was time for their honeymoon.

Niagara Falls was their choice.
Then they rented a Rolls Royce.

The happy couple stayed on the Canadian side,
Then took that beautiful car for a ride.

They checked in at a fancy hotel.
Both were thrilled; you could tell.

The accommodations were just right.
Dining and dancing every night.

If one goes close to the Falls,
Be sure to stay behind the walls.

The newlyweds agreed that in married life,
They won't encounter any strife.

Summer

Everyone has their own reason.
Most agree it's our favorite season.

Fun activities are not few.
There is always something one can do.

Take a swim. Take a hike.
Hit the trail on your bike.

Take a stroll in the park.
Just don't stay after dark.

You can spend a day at the beach;
Just down the road within your reach.

Hop on a hot air balloon,
Up so high you can touch the moon.

How about a fun road trip?
Just remember, you can't take a nip.

Float your boat on a lake.
Family and friends you can take.

A fun thing to do is waterski.
Strength and balance are the key.

Fireworks in the summer sky;
Must be the 4th of July.

Wishing this time would last.
Looking back, we had a blast.

4ᵗʰ of July

Besides Christmas, it's our favorite holiday.
You can hear the revelers shouting HOORAY!
Of course, there will be fireworks.
It truly is a glorious day.

Can't forget why we celebrate
On this very important date.
Remembering those brave soldiers
Who secured our fate.

Driving through the neighborhood,
American flags look so good.

Jefferson penned the Declaration,
Well known for his dedication.

Colonists longed for independence,
The only thing that made any sense.

Patriots engaged in a revolution.
Defeating the British was the solution.
Saratoga, the turning point of the war,
Crushed our enemy to the core.

Finally, we all were free.
With God's help, it will always be.

Autumn

Let's make one thing clear:
Autumn is my favorite time of year.
Now that I'm twenty-one,
Going to an Octoberfest and drink some beer.

Deciduous trees turn yellow and red;
A beautiful sight often said.

It's time for easy living;
Looking forward to Thanksgiving.

Some folks may call me a loon,
Gazing at the harvest moon.

Apples and pumpkins are aplenty.
Cider and donuts suit my fancy.

This season is often called fall.
I truly think it's best of all.

Thanksgiving

There's a time in late November,
Not far from Christmas in December.

We take a break from everyday living,
And celebrate a day called Thanksgiving.

We open our doors to friends and family.
This wonderful gathering sure pleases me.
A dinner with turkey, stuffing, and pie…
No one loves it more than I.

There's one thing this feast demands.
Say a prayer and all hold hands.

Giving thanks is apropos;
The only way that we know.

Naturally, everyone is in a great mood…
The day to show our gratitude.

No need to do any guessing.
God has showered us with His blessing.

Let's all meet again next year.
Maybe some will shed a tear.

COVID

The world has encountered a heinous beast.
It was born in the Far East,

Causing sickness and death in its wake,
More deadly than an earthquake.

There is no place in which to hide.
Thousands of people have already died.

If only one could find a place,
Wouldn't need a mask to cover their face.

Researchers and chemists are all over the map,
Working all day; never taking a nap.

I believe the day will come.
Savvy doctors sure aren't dumb.

It's very difficult to endure.
With God's help, we'll find a cure.

Winter

We've been waiting all year.
Winter is finally here.

Skiers pray for snow.
The slopes are where they want to go.
It's really a great pastime,
More exciting than you may know.

Skaters wait for the cold,
An activity that never grows old.
Holding hands with your squeeze,
More fun in a chilly breeze.

We can't wait for Christmas Day.
It always promises to be gay.

Another holiday is quite near.
We'll be wishing each other Happy New Year.

How about a ride on a one-horse sleigh?
It will surely make your day.

Winter is called a wonderland,
And I've always been a fan.

War in Ukraine

What's happening in Ukraine
Can only be described as insane.
Sovereignty doesn't mean a thing
When dealing with Russia's war machine.

Murderous plans were hastily made.
Then Vladimir chose to invade.

Outnumbered, outgunned in the midst;
Still the patriots do resist.

Bombing and shelling add to its demise.
And all you hear are the children's cries.

Ukrainians aren't accustomed to killing.
Faced with combat, they're quite willing.

Destruction and chaos far and wide,
Praying God is on their side.

Bullets and shrapnel falling like rain,
Causing death and unbearable pain.

Ukraine borders the Black Sea.
Looking out Russian gunboats are all they see.

Resembling a deadly disease…
So many causalities.

The enemy commandeered half their grains,
Inducing hunger as it wanes.

The holocaustic killing of civilians in this war;
Something the free world will not ignore.

Refugees found safety in a neighboring land,
Thanks to the kindness of the Balkans and Poland.

Clothing, food, and shelter…
What these friendly people have to offer.

Longing to return to the land they love,
Praying for some help from above.

No one knows what the future will hold.
It won't happen without the brave and the bold.

First Responders

You crashed your car into a truck.
Now you're surely out of luck.

Emergency vehicles quickly appear,
Hoping to relieve some of your fear.

First responders immediately react.
Highly trained; that's a fact.

As they call for an ambulance,
They perform first-aid, making good sense.

Racing to the nearest hospital,
Doctors deem recovery is possible.

It would be a miracle if he'd survive.
Thank the Lord, he's still alive.

His condition was severe.
He wondered if death was near.
A team of surgeons made it clear
From now on, he has nothing to fear.

Lesson learned; he'll wear a seatbelt,
Avoiding another tragedy that he's been dealt.

We graciously thank the EMT,
Smartly performing their duty consistently.

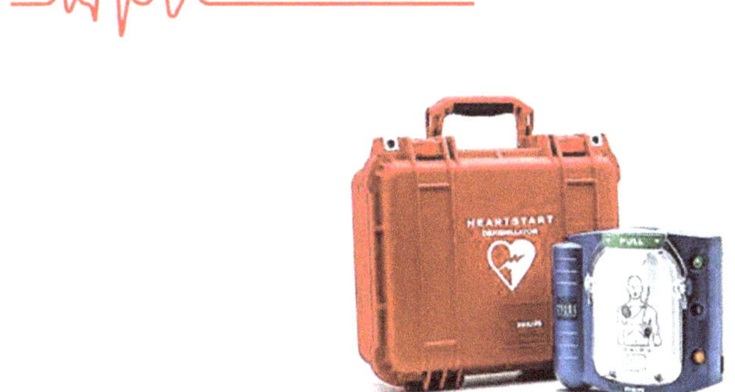

Firemen

There's a fire station in every city.
If there wasn't one, would be a pity.
These municipalities are always present;
A sense of safety for every resident.

When the 911 bell rings,
Quick response is what it brings.

Combating a raging fire can be dangerous.
For the looky-loos, it is obvious.

These brave men deserve honor and respect.
Knowing this, we can't forget.

We can be sure they'll do their duty;
The way it will always be.

Well trained at fighting fires,
Only the best will be hired.

As we sleep through the night,
Certain these men are doing what's right.

If one of them dies in their sleep,
We pray to God his soul to keep.

Inflation

It's a worldwide tragedy.
How it all began is not a mystery,
Referring to this high inflation,
A quick resolution is necessary.

This ugly situation is out of control.
It certainly has taken a toll.

Clothing, food, and gasoline
The highest prices we've ever seen.
As disturbing as it is for you and me,
Our cost of living has risen exponentially.

One of the culprits is Vladimir Putin,
As perversive as he's ever been.
He's partly responsible for this struggle.
Now we're shouldering a heavy burden.

Perhaps our president is partly to blame.
He shut down Alaskan oil which is a shame.

Now's the time to turn the page.
At this point it's taken center stage.

Heads of State are brainstorming,
Searching for an end to this thing.
At this time we're anxiously coping,
Praying for a solution they might bring.

They may provide a reason for thanks.
Only then could we fill our tanks.

It's quite evident that we care.
Maybe we should all say a prayer.

Hoping that our anxious plea,
Will lead to a fait accompli.

Homelessness

Hard to believe millions are homeless in this country;
A nationwide civic tragedy.
Poverty is a separate issue;
Referring to people wallowing in misery.

Most certainly a disheartening situation,
Leaving citizens sinking in desperation.

Many cities have at least one shelter.
Still, there are reasons to swelter.

Not like they committed a crime.
Great majority don't have a dime.

All they own are the clothes on their back.
They'd settle to sleep in a run-down shack.

Trying to find something to eat
Likens to climbing a rocky hill in bare feet.

Searching for work is horrific.
Offered a job, they'd accept in a New York minute.

Reluctant to admit defeat;
Still can stand on two feet.

Some had jobs; then given the boot.
Now they're stuck without any loot.

Stumbling around with empty pockets…
Recalling poor choices and regrets.

If things hadn't gone so wrong,
They wouldn't be singing such a sad song.

Praying for means to survive…
A depressing time to be alive.

A small number succumbed to alcohol and drug
     addiction.
Adding more harm to their current condition.

A few chose criminal activity.
It goes on in every city.
They're not much concerned;
Already lost their dignity.

It would take a Herculean effort
To provide a measure of comfort.

The problem has become critical.
A favorable ending would take a miracle.

Racism

Racism is a word that's bandied about.
Heard every day…without a doubt.

We all deserve our dignity.
Less than that is a travesty.

We welcome immigrants,
Not deserving of hateful rants.

Perpetrators should reconsider their belief,
And save these people from their grief.

Strapped with a painful stigma…
Coping with a lifelong dilemma.

This tragedy affects more than a few.
A blessed ending is long overdue.

African Americans have a slogan.
They're disturbed why it all began.
They 'spouse that Black Lives Matter.
It's time to act and not just chatter.

These disparaging feelings can't go on.
Maybe there's a resolve we'll happen upon.

Now's the time to end this behavior.
It would be in everyone's favor.

Mass Shooting

We must discover a way for this to stop;
Maybe better training for the cops.

These murderous shootings are indeed
The very last thing that we need.

Gun control is one of the ways
A crazy environment happening these days.

There's no need for automatic weapons.
Our sense of security has been threatened.

Post a guard in the school's doorway,
And protect our children every day.

Background checks could help out.
Perhaps Joe Biden could muster his clout.

He could use his executive power.
We've already reached the eleventh hour.

Everyone knows he can talk.
Now's the time to walk the walk.

The shooting in Texas disturbed all of us.
Twenty-one people were thrown under the bus.
It surely shook our sense of trust.
A hot topic the authorities must discuss.

We all hope for sanctuary.
Then we won't need to be so wary.

This hideous activity can't go on.
We hope there's a resolution they'll happen upon.

Everyone wishes to end this behavior.
Maybe we could pray for help from our Savior.

Wild West

I recall the brave lawmen
Who chased outlaws from 6 till 10.
They were diametrically opposed.
The way it was way back when.

The Earp Brothers tamed Tombstone.
You'd never see them working alone.

They won that gunfight at the O.K. Corral,
With Doc Holliday's help who was their pal.

A legend in the Old West was Wild Bill,
Playing poker when he was killed.
The hand he held was Aces & Eights.
Now he's buried on Boot Hill.

A bank and train robber was Jessie James.
Also known by several names.
A dirty little coward shot Mr. Howard,
Leaving his gang miserably lame.

New Mexico gave us Billy the Kid.
Robbery and murder is what he did.

Began his rampage at age 21.
Was only 12 when he holstered a gun.

John Wesley Hardin was the worst of all;
Killed 46 men; some for no reason a'tall.

Shot a man because he snored.
The bullet went through him…lodged in a bed
        board.

Hardin received the governor's decision…
Seventeen years in a hot Texas prison.

His six-shooter he laid down.
Then began to turn his life around.
Became a famous lawyer,
Touted as the best in town.

There's definitely more to say.
Suppose I'll save it for another day.

Born on April 29, 1947, in Troy, New York, Mīchol Zampier continues to make Troy his home. Mīchol graduated from School 18 with the highest marks in his graduating class. As an accomplished handicapper unless Saratoga Race Course moves, it's Troy to the finish line.

Being adventurous and restless by nature, Mīchol gravitated toward a variety of work environments. His artistic qualities know no bounds, taking him to interior decorating, winning dancing contests, Fred Astaire ballroom dance instructor, to gourmet chef and waiter extraordinaire.

Mīchol has a congenial, witty, and engaging personality and added his own brilliance and flair in all his professions. Oh, you would have relished being at his table at La Serre, the finest French restaurant in Albany, New York. Tableside Caesar salad, flaming Strawberries Romanoff, or torched Bananas Foster, anyone? Let's not forget Crêpes Suzette.

In retirement, Mīchol keeps his mind active and alert by studying the races of the day and placing his virtual "picks" on his extensive paper log. And he rarely misses his favorite show, *Jeopardy*.

Edit/Artwork support: Linda Deane, Nancy Szews
Content other than poems: Linda Deane